Better Living through Cats

poems by

Clark A. Pomerleau

Finishing Line Press
Georgetown, Kentucky

Better Living through Cats

Publisher: Leah Huete de Maines

Editor: Christen Kincaid

Cover Art: John Thompson

Author Photo: Clark A. Pomerleau, self-portrait at John A. Finch Arboretum
in Spokane, Washington

Cover Design: Elizabeth Maines McCleavy

Order online: www.finishinglinepress.com
also available on amazon.com

Author inquiries and mail orders:
Finishing Line Press
PO Box 1626
Georgetown, Kentucky 40324
USA

Table of Contents

*Cette poésie est dédiée
à ma famille
féline et humaine choisie.*

*Special gratitude to Diane R. Wiener, Marie C. Jones,
and Barbara Oglesby Rodman
for their support.*

poems composed between December 2017 and October 2019

Curls

My body is the box you fit yourself into each night
silky fur pressed my torso's length
forepaws fill cupped hand
feathery tail tip curls absently around my wrist
purrs throb through Scout's ribbed bed frame
humming in rhythm with my strokes
contentment entering spaces
like atoms exchanging electrons
in harmonious love
head weighed down with sleep
a velvet rock pillowed on bicep
old grey silhouette in twilight
Safe

Ley Line

Honey walks gingerly across grass
following a remnant path
steppingstones long gone
nobody else would see a difference
among blades
sensing deeper
she always picking that route
feels the ley line

Blended Family

Blended family sisters
nose each other
through windows
race house lengths
posture and lunge
behind glass

They meet in the middle
room enough but one
too pampered
for feral freedom

Foundations shift, re-order
new young one
repeats the performance
mirrors outer sis
shadows inner sib

Now that the door won't click shut
baby slips out to seize the porch
every chance she gets
goes limp as I
bring her back in
to spoil

First Time

She follows me to bed
flops down
like our first time
is routine
My arms encircle her
tentative air hug
She nudges her head onto my hand
throat vibrating affection
paws hugging back

Grandmothers

1.

You come back to me
wet dust scent on a breeze
my brain has labeled
'mothballs'
since distant explorations of
closets and trunks.
Frequent wisps of you
intimate connection to
heat and humidity
and yearning
Time cannot blunt.

2.

I see you in the cheeks and noses
of east Texas and north Louisiana.
Women far too young
your mediums
to the ghost of a child
in my head.
If their jowls speak in your grammar
I am fully possessed with
your presence.

3.

You crossed back to me
through a vivid dream:
I mirrored your hairstyle
happy.
You had a last gift for me
polished rocks
spread glimmering on the coffee table
like precious metals
pulsating
with your love.

4.

In pilgrimages home
to extra R's in Warshington
I hear you.
In flashes of emotional genius
I channel you.
You never speak through others in this world;
old Nashville accent
stamped out by time.
But your ephemera surrounds me.

Sacred Space

Honey rests rapt by the altar statue
while I uproot bunches of tall grass
lift up venerable pavers
A charcoal snake races away
frogs hop reluctantly
displaced from their sacred space
by landscape cloth, blocks, gravel
The animals will return
disturbed and unappreciative of
severe serenity for the sage
flanked by elephants ears
and overseen by vertical pupils

Conditions

What happens in a small child
when the menfolk drop around her
when Marys age prematurely
into three generations of widows
creased by deaths, fire
shell-shocked conversationalists
Deflected violence leaks acid on generations

Under tension to put away tomboy liberty
like so much rabbit weed
and mature from tom to proper lady Mary
grown terribly superior but oh so humble
the perfect noblesse-obligé
for an aspiring white-collar husband
who built a home
he never had claim to own

How hard to be a regular guy
Flint surrounded by steel women
and dams
whose male kittens couldn't survive
in years of litters
tomhoods refused

Better living through cats
queered manhood isolate
Flint's lot, an inheritance
passed to a grateful heir

But his daughters pushed
to polish their mirrors
glinting opposites
from namesakes' bond
polarized to repel
attracted to wed
or pulled to run
away

Pitiful queen befriended
another Mary, displaced newlywed
worried about the latest war
having to return home
to the widow realm
where its new queen bonded with Auntie
banished to the basement
while her runt traveled on

Conditions for grief,
depression, anxiety, perfection
pass from house to home
as inherited culture
auric tears that kept
the runt at the door
deciding whether to come or go

Swaddled tight in white
despite Pinky Lady and Blue Boy guards
the new one wriggles loose to finger paint
an earthy dreamscape
exuberant at her window to mess
transgression marks her though
she's too young to confess

Parents marveled
at producing a gay youth
the skipping tomboy
felt father's contentment
beneath the stoic melancholy
under mother's dis-ease
the house would recall its own

Minds and feet fly
to lush corners
where mud squishes to re-mind
garter snakes slither
in greens so bright
our old selves reignite

Untended

Travel until the country road winds
to the watermelon patch.
Untended seeds sprout where you rooted.
I'll snip the fence to gulp down my juicy past
gnaw to the rind.

The wind sighs in Grandma's
finger-wagging tongue
"Boy, you are such a worry wart."
Gusts around in the mind
how an abscess made
a happy-go-lucky babe ruminate.

Her generation dead a decade.
Every cell in us is new.
You have lived well beyond this patch.
Past care breaks down melon to rebuild me.

Left Behind

A terrified cat, cooped up with her nemesis, bolted
into the woods the instant
Mom tried to comfort her
counted on the kindness of strangers
in houses yards from midland groves
knowing Callie would not return to an enemy
another connection gone
like Raggedy Andy slumped in a gas station
we left behind everyone I knew

Generational Trauma

What are the odds of a drunk driver hitting a small boy in 1926?

Smashing that one of 14,000
where there were more trees than people?

Brothers' play cut short
limp toddler carried in
laid out at home
to die surrounded by family.
The second child Mémé and Pépé buried.
So hard to fathom.

A glimmer of depth
over eighty years later
grieving older brother says,
"It should have been me."

Haunted, Grandpa also died at home
with family who tried to care for him
but couldn't mend his wounds.

Unraveling

Just one thread unknotted
a tiny space unstitched
the smallest frayed edge

Lost words,
misattributed motives,
events renarrated

Like a silenced debater
a (not) stolen clock
a nice young man
no other loved one saw.

I reappear
again, again, again
at the unraveling.

Torn Apart

We watch through the rainy window
a bird too big to hunt
heavy scavenger settles on roadkill
peels off strips of flesh
methodically rends sinews and tendons
to gulp down remains
while showers wash over it all.

Being torn apart.
Grief does its slow job
cleans up messy emotions
strips back to
gleaming bones of lost love.

The first time I saw my father cry
was at his brother's funeral
The last when our visit ended.
A trickle overflowed the eye's gutter.
I used to build up to cathartic tears.
That dried up with manhood.

Writing now the talon and storm
that pound the rhythm of distress
give voice so it doesn't choke me.

What Do You Do (Ode to Rev. Fred Rogers)

What do you do with the grief that you feel
when the loss feels like a big hole
everything plunges in and there is
no one to pull you out and console.

Do you have a good cry
or distract yourself?
Do you sit with the pain 'til you know
that it is not you, and it will go?

It's best to remember that feelings subside.
It won't always be as it has been.
Try not to miss the good from before
new worth will come back to you again.

River

Burbles
from thin aired source

ice melt threatens
to freeze   You numb

Tributaries sweep in debris
clog
slow swelling flow
to an exhausted trickle

Water remains
        Flexible
              Enduring
                    In constant motion

              A burgeoning cascade

              So Powerful
            You can cut stone
            from Your path to
          come into Your essence

Torrent Projections

The curtain of rain
pushed up the street leaving
drenched cars, pavement, people
Wishing itself a forest torrent
that moved through trees
as a wet wall
quaking the aspen
whipping the willows
dripping from each needle
to replenish the streams
instead of flowing into ditches
Yet, witnessed with awe
by the man in soaked socks

The pressure headache broke
when the sky opened
simultaneously so beautiful
verdant magnified
while deepening mud
I sink down
hoping when the rainfall lessens
sucking stuck will slacken

As the sunset claws at the horizon
scrabbles to keep his head above
the storm warning
the man asks, "Did the Sun forsake us?"
Left to crashing winds
projections of Nature flash across
ego's screen
clinging fear fatigues
wooden from whittling
another embodied metaphor
outsized wood acorn
a smooth fidget pacifier

Nature Managed

If I'm honest
I like nature managed
more than wild
Raw power elicits fearful respect
but taming builds trust and need

Pockets of uncut forest
cast long shadows too
from grim fairy tales
that warned: woods kill
with natural predators
and unknowns
myths made of the Fay
not Tinkerbell and fairy dust
but changlings and enslavement

Summers at parks
that cultivated managed nature
cemented my love of
Japanese gardens
the lanterns amid carefully staged flora
in the created pond basins
imagine feline delight as
fish rise to greet you

Labor Day

Crouched you peer unseen through
a gap in the fence
Workers spent a week
enclosing land
already marked off by bird-shat trees
and abutting neighbors
The fence you dug underneath
before the gate stopped shutting

Eyes track back and forth as he
mows down rows of grass
swears while piling up rocks
Sisyphus undoing his predecessor's labor
bemusing
manufactured problems

He only comes out to leave or
alter something
What is he missing
while so fixated?
You turn, attention honed
on small game

Live on the Brim

Pour coffee and cream
to the brim
Inhale stacks of chocolate
gifts from him
Reject moderation
for stroking soft fur
so pleasure yields
hours of purr
Read to learn more
ever eager to know
Visit the garden daily
eyes do not overflow

Anxiety Dreams

Fitfully dozed nights
curled up
all elbows, knees, and ankles
limbs unspool to relax
to shake out ache
strained calm betrayed by the body

Nightly I spit out teeth
losing what should be firm
to the familiar wiggle of childhood
cracked or pristine molars pop out
into a basin
while I watch in the mirror

a window to another recurring dream
where everyone I care about
surrounds my bed
to tell me how disappointed they are in me
I still see the priest's letter
harsh words spilt all over the envelope

I can feel the paper cutting
Only I've spent years
piling up successes
sandbagged against such floods
with mindfulness and
brushing three times a day

Street lamp muscles aside stars
to pierce the gap in the curtains
from midnight lull to groggy sunrise
dark edges of life's
stacked afterthoughts tumble
idle dreams into a forgotten abyss.

Prey

Crouch, wiggle butt, pounce
quick detangle bounce
from each one-sided tango

How many lifeless geckos
will bury themselves here
tails wriggling echoes?

I warn the praying mantis
not to enter drear
another plaything

Nothing Much

Beneath the hissing frother
yowls for milk punctuate
the sound of typing
one writes
the other begs
with nothing much to hunt
years of domestication
sharpen wit
cup batted off the table
cries
spilt milk

That the Sun Also Rises

you bolt awake
the sun struggles to rise
billowing sheets portend
bleach black to blue-grey
last star a winking night light
over silhouette trees that
endure their bogey costumes
not yet stripped to reveal
unique leaves folded
in morning prayer

roused feral paces
on a shingled perch
pale imitation of a lynx
meowing, since you're up
the glaring generations
assemble, cast aside
ambivalence
for primal need
insatiable
like your daily reassurance
that the sun also rises

Seneca Prayer

Fearless cat
imagines comfort and cheer
names herself Seneca.
Conjured cat
bats at the corners of joy
avoiding what may never
occur.

So unlike poor Hothead,
boys-will-be-man's
nonconsensual chase
made skittish.
Weathered kitten cowering
before false shadows of evil.
Find the company
of women
who shut out such men
and take in "too many" cats.

May the cowed return
rebirthed through Seneca
immaculate conception.
Hope, favored kitten,
always fully living.

Messenger

From warm circling sun
ears prick, pound
a sacred hum. Sparkling
a snowy line darts
across the gap
the gap bridged
bows wiggling tail, false
cognate to playful.
White streak tackles me
knocks away whispered
domestication, enters
called and welcomed
gifts delicate. Muzzle reveals
sharp words. Dive in.
Emanate. Cunning, desperate
need against deception.
The tail vanishes,
leaving wisps of ethereal fur
on my skin.

Grief

Grief hangs limp

a cat forced aloft
submits to petting
before she gets
what she wants

squirms impatient
scratches and bites
until you can't wait
to put it down

Grounding

A round-faced moon
shines out of the abyss.
Yank the curtains closed
to shut out glare on woe.
Heart pounding, grope to recline.
Cannot let the flood drown me.

Wide eyes grow scratchy.
Squeeze them tight but pant,
wheeze, gasp,
as waves engulf and pound
a suffocating weight
onto my chest.

Her lithe step grounding me,
the cat leaps to my side.
Brushing against my heaving ribs,
she offsets this tension,
turns, curls up,
hums.

Calming vibration,
warm back,
a satisfied stretch,
drapes paws
like reiki on pulse points,
tail flicking against my fingers.

Motor to lull,
Twitching paws tell me
she is already asleep
chasing in her dreamscape.
I long to bat at sunbeams.
Or at least share careless rest.

A Lighter Load

Scratch to cover
as Archie Bunker
flushes delight
Ka-chunka-chunka-chunk
down stairs
victory lap
at a lighter load

Cast-off Self

Cast-off self
locks knotted
around clippings
make a doll
knitting spells
breathe life
into keratin

I'd weave it
clothes of valerian
and lavender
to rest well
before victory
at the floral game
gold violet or
silver marigold to reap

but the cat would leap,
absconder
smother the prey's
misery
keep it from fame
knocked under
the dresser junk heap

Better to flush detritus
to break down elsewhere
and hug the cat
unmoving dreams

Spilt Cat

Two bottles of cat spilt
on every flat surface
blown out rubber melted
into hot asphalt

lethargy lurks
then cat harbingers
of frisking cooler times

Somehow, they know

The House Expands

At table
hand clasp glee
multi-course joy
feeds you
to embody your power

Flutter swallowtail
against asphalt
moth chase
to safety tree
shot in green

The house expands
inhaling love
cat follows
tail encircling calf
chittering about progenitors

Clark A. Pomerleau has folded commitments to history, observation, relationships, and regeneration into his lyric poetry. By mixing in a century of memories from places as varied as Washington, Maine, Tennessee, Louisiana and Texas, or Illinois, Pomerleau invites readers to consider the emotional landscape of inherited culture. He offers a world in which to explore the meanings of our feelings and dreams. Interactions among people, animals, plants, and rocks structure poetic stories. Warm present-day relationships reflect comfort we nurture while nature becomes another space of refuge and replenishment.

Inspired by Audre Lorde and Walt Whitman (among others), Pomerleau creates poetry as an economical art form that promotes conscious, sensory living, in order to develop our power. When the world seems shaky, the poems acknowledge pain instead of smothering emotions with platitudes. Recurring queer and trans images embrace authenticity and invite readers to value what makes them unique. Hope enters into Pomerleau's poetry like plant shoots pushing up from established roots, helping loss move through while inner work blossoms into resilience.